If I Could Change My Mom and Dad

If I Could Change My Mom and Dad

by
Bill Orr
and
Erwin Lutzer

MOODY PRESS
CHICAGO

Library of Congress Cataloging in Publication Data

Orr, Bill.
If I could change my mom and dad.

1. Parenting—Religious aspects—Christianity.
2. Parents—Religious life. 3. Family—Religious life.
4. Children—Religious life. I. Lutzer, Erwin W.
II. Title.
BV4529.066 1983 248.8'4 82-18848
ISBN 0-8024-0174-0

3 4 5 6 7 Printing/LC/Year 87 86 85 84 83

Printed in the United States of America

To
Cheryl, Joe, Sandra, Jackie, and Nancy Orr
and
Scott and Laurie Campbell

Contents

CHAPTER	PAGE
Preface	9
Introduction: The Value of a Child	13
1. Children Want Parents to Love Them	17
2. Children Want Parents to Listen to Them	30
3. Children Want Parents to Spend Time with Them	42
4. Children Want Parents to Respect Them	55
5. Children Want Consistent Discipline	71
6. Children Want Parents to Be Free from Stubborn Habits	81
7. Children Want Parents to Get Along	94
8. Children Want to Have Two Parents	105
9. Children Want Parents to Be Spiritual Leaders	116
10. Some Children Are Satisfied with Their Parents	128
Conclusion: A Child and His God	139

Preface

I want you to meet Bill Orr, the man known to children throughout the United States and Canada as "Uncle Bill."

Who is this man whom some children would like to adopt as their own father, who has held children's crusades in hundreds of churches and cities, and who receives a constant flow of letters from children enrolled in "The Mailbox Club"?

Born and raised in St. Louis, Missouri, Bill Orr was four years old when his father died and his grandparents adopted him. Even at such a young age he began to realize that his mother had rejected him.

"Billy, get ready! Your mother is coming, and she wants to love you!" his grandparents would say. So Billy would get ready in his clean white shorts and top. But when Mother arrived he would crawl under the bed or into the closet to hide. "After all," he reasoned, "if she loved me she'd raise me."

The boy grew up with a festering bitterness. Other kids talked about their moms and dads, but Billy was different. His mother didn't want him.

At the age of thirteen, Bill ran away from home, and when he was seventeen, he joined the Marines. Then, at twenty-one, he accepted Christ as his Savior. His grandfather had taught him about Christ before, but Bill had made only a shallow profession of faith until 1953, when he truly gave his trust to Jesus Christ.

Despite his resentment of his mother, Bill used every opportunity to witness for Christ. For thirteen years he ran the same mail route in St. Louis and befriended children along the way. Often he'd stop and tell a Bible story to a group of children at the corner. One day he counted forty-two children standing on the sidewalk or sitting on the grass. Many of them put their faith in the Lord Jesus Christ. Bill still keeps track of them today, as they actively serve the Lord.

Although God worked in Bill's life through the years, he still had not mastered that one sin: bitterness. Deep inside, his resentment toward his mother had not subsided. Then in March 1975 he attended a revival service. A Canadian preacher, Bill McLeod, was preaching on Galatians 2:20: "I have been crucified with Christ; and it is no longer I who live, but Christ lives in me."

Bill Orr fought with God. "Sure, I'm bitter, but remember, Lord, it's her fault. I didn't leave *her*. She left *me!*" But God was unconvinced. Bill learned that bitterness can never be justified. Never. Bitterness is sin, regardless of how badly we've been wronged. The Christian's example is Christ, who experienced injustice and responded by committing Himself to God. "While being reviled, He did not revile in return; while suffering, He uttered no threats, but kept entrusting Himself to Him who judges righteously" (1 Peter 2:23).

Finally, Bill could take it no longer. He confessed his sin and received God's cleansing from the resentment he had carried with him all those years. The next day he flew to Virginia to ask his mother to forgive him for his hostility about the past. The hurts of many years were finally healed.

With that experience came a new calling to share the good news about Christ's love with a wider audience. Today Bill continues to work with the post office in St. Louis, but he conducts Children's Booster Rallies on weekends. In his children's meetings, he asks the youngsters to complete this sentence: "If I could change my mom and dad, I would. . . ." Some of their revealing answers are found in this book.

What hurts Bill the most? Next to seeing children who are neglected or abused, it's when a child says to him, "I wish you were my dad." Bill knows that child is really crying, "I wish my mom and dad would listen to me. . . . I wish they'd really care."

You're in for a special experience as you read the honest and unedited replies of children, expressing how they feel about their own moms and dads. Perhaps in reading what these children have written you'll read between the lines. You might even find they have written about you!

Erwin Lutzer, Senior Pastor
The Moody Church
Chicago, Illinois

Introduction:

The Value of a Child

> Whoever receives one such child
> in My name receives Me.
>
> Matthew 18:5

When someone asked D. L. Moody how many people were converted at a meeting, he replied, "Two and a half."

"Two adults and a child, I suppose," the questioner continued.

"No," replied Moody, "two children and an adult. The children have their whole lives to live for Christ; the adult's life is half over."

Christ spoke with great compassion about children, displaying sensitivity and tenderness for those little ones. When the disciples asked, "Who then is the greatest in the kingdom of heaven?" He answered by calling a child to Himself, teaching the disciples that children enjoy a privileged place in God's program.

What characteristics do children have that attract God's attention? First, children are examples of the kingdom of heaven. Christ refers to their humility, their unpretentious and honest attitude. We have all noticed how children usually do not try to impress visitors; they do not hesitate to reveal embarrassing family secrets. They make no attempt to make prayers sound pious—whatever is on the inside comes out. Unless we humble ourselves as little children, we shall not enter the kingdom of heaven.

Children by nature believe and trust their parents. They never worry about the future if their parents assure them that all will be well. Their lack of pretense and simple faith ought to characterize us as well.

But because children are so open and trusting, they are easily misled. If the baby in his mother's arms is not taught about Christ's love—if he is taught to be indifferent about spiritual values—he will assume his parents are leading him correctly. Children desire to believe their parents; they want to behave like them, too. The qualities that make children so special also make them vulnerable.

Second, children bear a special relationship to Jesus Christ. "Whoever receives one such child in My name receives Me" (Matthew 18:5). If we don't receive our children as we should, we don't receive Christ as we should!

What does it mean to receive a child in Christ's name? Unfortunately, some children are received in the name of necessity and simply endured. Others are received in the name of pride—to continue the family name or have an outstanding career. Some are received in the name of selfishness; their parents take self-centered satisfaction in their own offspring. To receive a child in the name of Christ is to recognize that he is a gift whose care God has entrusted to us.

Consider the warning Jesus gives: "Whoever causes one of these little ones who believes in Me to stumble, it is better for him that a heavy millstone be hung around his neck, and that he be drowned in the depths of the sea" (Matthew 18:6). Think of the tragedy of children who refuse the Savior because their parents have let them stumble!

Christ warned that we should not despise one of these little ones—by neglect, lack of discipline, or inadequate love and affection. In all of these ways we are held accountable to God. A child stumbles easily, and we are responsible for guiding his footsteps along the path of life.

Finally, children have a special relationship to God the Father. "See that you do not despise one of these little ones, for I say to you, that their angels in heaven continually behold the face of My Father who is in heaven" (Matthew 18:10). Christ doesn't mean that children who die will become angels. He refers to guardian angels—"ministering spirits, sent out to render service for the sake of those who will inherit salvation" (Hebrews 1:14). The angels who have special charge for the children enjoy the nearest favor of God; they behold His face. Apparently, the highest angels guard the smallest subjects of God's kingdom!

What does all of this mean to parents? Christ says that it is better to live with unfulfilled desires than to cause your children to stumble. "It is better for you to enter life crippled or lame, than having two hands or two feet, to be cast into the eternal fire . . . it is better for you to enter life with one eye, than having two eyes, to be cast into the fiery hell" (Matthew 18:8-9). Put another way, Christ is teaching that *the fulfillment of any career or personal success can never compensate for neglecting a child.* Better to earn less money, to die unknown, to stop climbing the ladder of success, or to be maimed and blind, than to carelessly step on the little saplings God has given us to tend.

Let's turn our attention to the children—their joys, hurts, and questions—so that we can better guide their unsteady footsteps along the path of life.

1

Children Want Parents to Love Them

Behold, children are a gift from the LORD.

Psalm 127:3*a*

Girl — age 9:

If would change my Mom or Dad I would ask them to love me.

Girl — age 7:

I tell

them to

Love me

Boy — age 10:

I would have them love me more.

Girl — age 8:

I would ask them

to love me

more.

Girl—age 13:

If I could change my
momand dad I wouldn't
change my mom
I would change
my dad I would
Want him to read
the bible tome
Pray with me
Love god
connfes his sins
care for me
treet me equel
as mysisters
Love me and
not Bete me

Girl—age 14:

If I could change my mom and dad I would like for them to discipline me in love and not in anger. I would also like for them to show their love more each day. I would want them to just learn (know) how to Show lore instead of anger or impatience.

Boy—age 12:

~~Make them~~

Let them

be loving parents.

Girl—age 10:

If I could change
my Mom & Dad,
This is what I'd do,
I would ask them to
Love me in every
thing I do

P.S. except
when I do wrunge

Girl:

Dear Uncle Bill
I have al~~k~~ways
done what ~~the~~ other people
~~who~~ wanted and I have
done things that other
people want just be-
cause I wanted a friend
but I don't even have
a friend.

I think I got
baptized for my mother
and the chruch so I
maybe could feel love
but I never did

Girl—age 12:

If I could change my mom & dad I would teach them to hug & & tell me they love me. My parents never hug me. My older brother gets ALL the attention.

Some times I wish I would get real sick & mabey they would notice me.

I only wish they would hug me.

"If I could change my mom and dad, I'd have them love me all the time . . . not just when I'm good."

Parents may say, "I love my child," when we ought to say, "My child enriches my life." In other words, our love is often based on personal delight or pleasure. What happens when the child misbehaves or disappoints us—when we feel anger or hurt? Our real feelings show, and we end up demoralizing a child by saying, "Mother doesn't love naughty boys." The implication is clear: "When you no longer make me feel wonderful, your worth as a child disappears, and you're no longer worthy of my love."

Our conditional love is communicated to children in a hundred subtle ways—comparing one child with another, inconsistent discipline, and personal attacks. What we are really saying is, "How I feel determines whether I love you or not." The root is selfishness, a conditional acceptance depending on whether the child is an asset or a liability to the parent's feelings.

Divine love finds its roots in the person who can love *regardless of the response* in the one loved. In other words, the child's value never depends on his performance. Without divine love, a child is filled with anxiety, depression, and rebellion. He will misbehave, repeatedly testing his parents' love, groping for the assurance that he is loved, no matter what he does.

How can parents display unconditional divine love?

1. Put away all bitterness from our own lives.

Some parents cannot express love because they themselves were not loved. Until they have resolved their feelings toward their own parents, they will not be able to communicate love. Equally important, parents must confess the sin of rejecting an unwanted child. Regardless of the circumstances of his birth, the parents must accept the child as a gift from the hand of God.

2. Love and respect one another as parents. Couples cannot hide their conflicts from their children. And seeds sown in a bad marriage relationship usually bear fruit in the life of a child.

3. Communicate love to a child consistently and in a variety of ways. Though children often cannot understand words, they are sensitive to feelings—a voice, physical contact—children can pick up signals with unbelievable accuracy. I've had one of my children say, "Dad, why are you so upset?" when I had been confident that my feelings were securely hidden.

Let's give our children the divine and unconditional love they so desperately need.

2

Children Want Parents to Listen to Them

Let everyone be quick to hear, slow to speak, and slow to anger; for the anger of man does not achieve the righteousness of God.

James 1:19

Girl — age 10:

If I could change
my Dad
This Is what I
would Take
more time
with me. and
Listen to what
I say.

Boy — age 11:

If I could change my mom and dad I would make them listen when there working

Boy — age 15:

I would like
them to under
stand [redacted] more
about me, and
listen better,
and understand
why I listen to
the music,
and other things
I like to
listen to,

Girl—age 12:

Dear Uncle Bill,
IF I could change
my mom and dad
it would be hard what
to change them. But I
think I'd tell them to
listen to what I had
to say so they'd Know
that I agreed with
them so they would n't
have to say any
more.

Gail—age 11:

IF I COULD CHANGE MY MOM & DAD I WOULD PRAY THAT THEY WOULD SPEND MORE TIME WITH ME, & LISTEN TO ME MORE.

Girl — age 15:

If I could change my mom and dad i would have them talk to me more. My mother talks to me but it's not like the good close talking i really want. My father doesn't talk to me at all and i'd like a closer relationship with him. I would like to share my feelings with them and have them help me with my problems.

girl:

I wish Dad would talk to me

Girl—age 10:

If I could change my mom or dad. I'd make them listen to what I say because it might be important.

Girl—age 11:

IF I could change
my mom and
dad Id wan't
them to have
the time to
listen to me
and love me
as mush as
they could.

Why is good listening so important? First, it shows respect; it says that we believe our children are important. A child's hurts and joys are just as meaningful as an adult's ups and downs. Second, careful listening acquaints us with our children and gives them self-respect. Even rebellious teenagers have reversed their attitudes when their parents have begun to listen to what they say and try to understand their feelings.

Unfortunately, most of us don't know how to listen. But listening can be learned, if we all take time to see its importance and benefits to the family. Here are some pointers:

1. Direct eye contact is a primary means of communicating love, understanding, and self-esteem. Unfortunately, many parents use eye contact only when reprimanding a child—not when giving encouragement or approval. Without eye contact, a child will often become withdrawn and alienated from the adult world. Look at your child when he speaks.

2. Physical contact is an absolute necessity, if we want to show approval, build a relationship, and assure our children of our unconditional love.

3. Focused attention takes time, but it makes a child feel valuable and important in his parents' eyes. The most precious memories and lasting impressions a child may have are the moments spent with parents who can listen and talk freely with their children without distraction or righteous condescension.

Do you know your child? Have you listened carefully—not to give advice, but simply to identify with his emotions and desire to be loved? Take the time to make him feel he is the most important person in the world to you. Your child is waiting for you to hear what he has to say.

3

Children Want Parents to Spend Time with Them

"Permit the children to come to Me; do not hinder them; for the kingdom of God belongs to such as these." . . . And He took them in His arms and began blessing them, laying His hands upon them.

Mark 10:14*b*, 16

Girl—age 11:

If I could chage
my mom-DaD,
I ask them
to spen
some time
with me

Boy—age 7:

if I could change my mom and DAD I would. I would have them spend more time with me.

Boy—age 7:

if I chould chage my DaD to Play with me more oftin Because He Hardley Plays with me

Boy—age 14:

do more things with
kids cause he's
too busy always
meetings
etc.

Boy — age 9:

I would change my dad
that he would play
Hocky with me.

Boy—age 9:

Make my Dad
play baseball
on Saturday
from 1.00–3.30

Girl—age 11:

To spend more time with me. Teach me how to do things that I don't know how to do. Spend time doing sports.

Boy—age 10:

To bring me to more places and have more time to play with me

Boy — age 6:

If I could
cange my
mom
I wood ask her
to help me with
my school work.

Boy:

I wish my dad
didn'T have so
many meetings.
please pray pray
That my dad
won'T have
so many
meetings

Boy:

play with

me.

"Our parents have given us everything except themselves."

Often a child will misbehave simply because he craves attention. Even the physical pain of a whipping is more tolerable than the emotional pain of being ignored. Someone has said that no parent has a right to spank his child, unless he plays with him. The value of discipline is directly related to the quality of the relationship—the closer the relationship, the less need for discipline. A child who has attention will want to please his parents.

1. We must *schedule time* with our children. Nothing but an emergency should allow us to cancel an appointment with our children once it is made. Our promises must be kept, or a child's confidence in us will be damaged.

2. We must *become interested* in what our children are doing. There's no reason why we can't rekindle our childhood imaginations for the benefit of our children. Why shouldn't something be important to us, if it's important to them?

3. We must *begin today*. Once again, it boils down to a matter of priorities. Parents often resolve that they will spend more time with their children in the future—when the car is paid for, the house is renovated, and the bills stop coming in. But it never happens. If we are not spending time with our children now, we will not do it in the future, either. We must make our commitments now, and we must stick to them.

4

Children Want Parents to Respect Them

Fathers, do not provoke your children to anger; but bring them up in the discipline and instruction of the Lord.

Ephesians 6:4

Boy—age 10:

I'd like my Mom
and Dad to listen to
me as if I were
worth something.

Girl—age 12:

Mom: I would like her to listen to me more often and not ignore my questions. Not like her to make fun of things I say.

Dad: Like to get serious answers to my questions more often.

Girl — age 11:

If I could change
my mom and Dad
side: make them
less strict, make
them listen to what
I say before they
answer, make it
so they don't
assume the worst
all the time

Girl—age 12:

I would change them by letting my tell my sides of the story in stead of just telling their side.

Girl—age 15:

If I could change my mom and dad. I would like to be able to talk to my dad freely without being yelled at or being preached to.

My mom is just fine.

Girl — age 17:

to have a little
more trust in me.
to let me explain
how I feel about
things befor they
start yelling.

Girl—age 12:

If I could change my mom + dad I would want them to let me explain if they think I've done something wrong instead of spanking me right away

Boy:

make them more understanding of my ~~[illegible]~~ weaknesses.

Girl — age 11:

If I could change my mom and dad I'd make them realize I'm a person who has feelings to!

Girl—age 12:

I would change them by [redacted] letting me have my opinion in family discussions."

Girl—age 13:

If I could change my Mom and Dad I would change them by having them not favor one person more then the other but love each one of us the same.

Boy — age 10:

I would want the

to recognize me

as areal person

Boy — age 8:

I would Change Their adatude

Building self-esteem in a child is one responsibility that cannot be delegated to others. The task is too difficult and too personal to be handled without commitment and support. A child's world can be a vicious place; children call each other names and ridicule those who are weak or deficient. Unfortunately, many parents unintentionally do the same thing!

What can we do to help our children build self-esteem?

1. We must always accept a child for what he is—just as he is—rather than because of his performance or physical appearance. It's so easy to make our acceptance conditional, letting our child think we love him for *what he does*, rather than *who he is*. Although one child may truly be easier to love than another, we must *learn* to love, realizing that each child's self-esteem depends on our total acceptance.

2. We must try to understand a child—to think his thoughts and to see life from his standpoint. Often I've expected too much from my children, simply because I'd forgotten what I was like at their age. Understanding takes time; it involves giving a child attention and being a good listener.

3. We must discipline without damaging self-esteem. A child should not be humiliated in front of others, and he should not be disciplined without precise cause. Parents must realize the need for discipline that suits the offense and must be sensitive to a child's spirit.

4. We must convey respect by listening with undivided attention to what a child has to say.

A child who is loved but not respected may think, "Well, they love me because I'm their child, but I'm disappointing to them as a person. I'm not measuring up to their expectations." Parents have the responsibility of making their child feel like the most important person in the world; we must love him, respect him, and let him know he has personal worth.

5

Children Want Consistent Discipline

Train up a child in the way he
should go,
Even when he is old he will not
depart from it.
Proverbs 22:6

The rod and reproof give wisdom,
But a child who gets his own way
brings shame to his mother.
Proverbs 29:15

Boy — age 11:

I would make them be slow to get angry.

Girl – age 8:

ASK THEM TO SPANK

ME WHEN I'M BAD.

Boy — age 10:

I would tell them

not too hit us and

give us a second

chance.

Girl—age 12:

I would like ~~them~~ to
see there is a difference
between be good
parents & being overly
strict parents. they
think that if they
a nice to you they
aren't being good.
Most parents listen
to there kids &
try to understand.
Mine don't.

Boy — age 11:

I would ask
them to
be more Payshunt
with me.

Boy—age 17:

If I could change my mom or dad, how would I change them? I love them greatly, and I see no great faults. They're great. I think my mom needs to enforce her rules a bit more (esp. on my brothers).

Girl—age 12:

I don't want to change my mom and dad. I like them the way they are except I would like my dad not to get so angry sometimes when there is no really no reason for it.

A woman reared in a home with no father and a negligent mother said she wished that her mother would speak to her more often; she wanted the security of knowing that her mother actually cared about her—enough to set some limits. When she would leave the apartment to play she sometimes called back, "OK, Mother, I'll be back at five o'clock." She knew her mother wasn't there. "I just spoke to nothing," she recalls. "I wondered what it would be like to have someone care when I'd be back." It was frightening for a five-year-old to know that nobody really cared when she returned from play. She had no instructions, no warnings, and no discipline. At the age of five she was on her own.

Disciplining a child is a sign of love. As the Scriptures teach, "FOR THOSE WHOM THE LORD LOVES HE DISCIPLINES" (Hebrews 12:6*a*). Since children crave love they also crave discipline; they desire the security of knowing that their parents love them enough to build some fences, to give some guidelines to keep them out of trouble.

Parents often fail because of permissiveness. The child is allowed to do whatever he pleases unless he infringes on the plans or whims of his parents. He's left to guess what is right and what is wrong, for it all depends on the mood of his parents. Such a child will deliberately misbehave, just to see if there's *anything* that will arouse his parents' ire. The thought that they don't love him enough to give restraints is fearful; he's his own boss in a world he isn't able to handle.

Overdiscipline is equally destructive. Some children are spanked (beaten?) for the smallest infractions—childish neglect, spilled milk, or irresponsibility. When a child misbehaves with real defiance, his parents have no suitable response except to spank him even harder. Physical punishment should be reserved only for serious offenses.

Inconsistency is probably the major failure of most parents. We've all known days when our children could get by with practically anything; then without warning, we were tempted to become angry and spank them for behavior that was apparently acceptable the day before. Discipline depends on the mood of the moment. In such instances we are actually acting like children—for we are out of control just as they are.

A child might say, "Look how my mother and father do exactly what I do. I stomp my little foot, and my father stomps his big foot. I threaten to punch him with my little fist, and he threatens to punch me with his big one." Thus the parent is reduced to the role of a child, since both are out of control.

Let's remember that a child sees his parents as a symbol of justice, stability, and wisdom. He looks to them for consistency and guidance. He wants the assurance that they can be trusted to do what is right and have his best interests at heart. When he has misbehaved he expects loving, fair, and consistent discipline. Only then does he know that he is truly loved.

6

Children Want Parents to Be Free from Stubborn Habits

I will not be mastered by anything . . . . Do you not know that your body is a temple of the Holy Spirit who is in you, whom you have from God, and that you are not your own? For you have been bought with a price: therefore glorify God in your body.

1 Corinthians 6:12*b*, 19-20

Girl – age 15:

I'd put my
mom on a diet.

Boy — age 9:

If I could change my mom and dad I would stop my dad from eating sweets and my mom from drinking coffee.

Girl — age 10:

If I could change
my mom & dad
what would I do?
Make my mom
skinnier and both
my mom & dad not
argue and make
them both healthier.

Girl – age 10:

I would ask them to go to church steady. and ask them to stop smoking.

Girl—age 9:

I'd help my Dad
stop drinking
and my mom
stop yelling and
being mad all
the time.

Girl—age 12:

If I could change my mom and Dad I would wish and pray that my dad would not drink or smoke and loved the lord.

Girl:

I wish my dad would start brushing his teeth so they wouldn't ~~had~~ be so yellowish.

Boy—age 11:

If I could change my mom and Dad I would try and try to make them stop smoking, if that didn't work I would pray to the Lord Jesus and ask for help from him.

Girl – age 10:

I would MAKE my
DAD STop smoKING
because IT gests
stuffy IN THE
HousE

Girl—age 11:

If I could change
my dad I would
stop him from
smoking and
swearing and
(swearing)
if I can change
my mom I would
take her temper away.

One afternoon in Chicago, I had my heart wrenched within me. I passed a father and his little girl, perhaps six years old. The man staggered, unable to walk upright. When he came to a tree, he stopped and leaned against it to regain his equilibrium. Clearly he was drunk—one of millions of alcoholics.

I shall never forget the terror I saw on the little girl's face, as she stood beside her daddy, waiting for him to gather his wits and continue to stagger down the street. Scores of people hurried by, oblivious to the familiar sight of a man too intoxicated to walk. Amid the heavy traffic, the little girl was alone. She probably could never have found her way home alone, so she had to wait for "Daddy," and Daddy didn't know where he was. I will never forget her anxious face.

That little girl may be living on your street. A conservative estimate indicates that there are twelve million alcoholics in the United States. What can parents learn from the comments of children like these?

1. Children are aware that vices such as drinking and smoking are harmful and degrading. They like to think that their parents have everything under control. To see them enslaved by a habit beyond their control breeds insecurity and shame. Children may eventually lose respect for their parents.

2. A parent's sins are often passed on to his children. A child cannot escape the influence of his parent's example. Ironically, the child who despises his parent's addiction will often end up in the same

slavery, concluding that "there must be no other way to live."

How can a parent who uses alcohol persuade his son not to use drugs?

It's difficult to live in bondage and preach freedom. If we expect our children to be morally free, then we must set the example.

7

Children Want Parents to Get Along

And be kind to one another, tender-hearted, forgiving one another, just as God in Christ also has forgiven you.

Ephesians 4:32

Girl—age 17:

I would have them love each other more, and get along better.
I would have my dad want to enter into more family devotions and fun times.

Boy — age 13:

If I could change
my mom and dad,
I would tell them not
to argue so much.

Girl – age 8:

IF I COUlD Change my MOM AND DAD I'd ask them to stop fighting and my mom to stop yelling.

Girl—age 8:

If I could change my dad I would make him not to be so mad at my family.

Girl—age 8:

Make Them Not To fight

Girl – age 8:

If I could cange my mom + dad I would ask my Mom + Dad not to fite

Boy—age 10:

I'd do something so they wouldn't fight

Girl—age 11:

I'd like my dad to stop smoking Sometimes I wake up in the night and hear my mom + Dad arguing. This doesn't happen often but I'd like in to stop.

Girl:

I hope some
day they would
stop fighting
and be kind to
the rest of us.
I get hurt
very very very
very much.
Dear God help
them.

A child cannot develop emotional security in a home that is torn by strife and disagreement. God intended for children to have the affection of parents who are one—physically, emotionally, and spiritually.

Think of what strife between a father and a mother does to a child. First, the child has no model, no guide after which he can pattern his life. Second, tension breeds insecurity. The child receives the message that love is conditional—"If Mommy can't love Daddy, will she stop loving me, too?" Third, the child is often forced into the terrible position of having to choose between his parents, or to take sides in the dispute. Uncontrolled anger ruptures the relationship between marital partners. After verbal abuse, something is lost that can never be regained. The effects on the child are devastating.

Parents must learn to love one another. Someone has said, "The greatest contribution a man can make to his child is to love the child's mother supremely." Love and security between parents will give the child the emotional security he will need to face adult life.

We can't save all the homes in America. But perhaps you can save one—your own. If love has drained from the marriage, learn to love one another. Make Christ the focus of your home—for His sake, for your sake, and for the sakes of those precious little ones God has given you.

8

Children Want to Have Two Parents

Above all, keep fervent in your love for one another, because love covers a multitude of sins.
1 Peter 4:8

Gil:

I love you very much! We have a terrible problem in our house!!!! The problem is: Dad has filed for divorce, but my mom does not want it. Plus she can't stop the divorce. We even went to Illinois for counciling. Please pray very hard for us. It is especialy hard for me because I'm the only one who wants to go with mom and I can't cause she's not my blood mother. Thanks bunches.

(P.S. Please write back!!!!)

Boy—age 11:

I would like to get my Parants back togethar aganc because they ar seperated. I reay like my and Dad togathar

Girl — age 12:

IF I COULD CHANGE MY MOM I PROBLEY WOULDN'T. IF I COULD CHANGE MY DAD I WOULD WANT HIM TO BE NICER AND NOT SO MEAN AND I WANT HIM TO BE MORE NICE TO MY MOM AND TO LIKE HER SO HE COULD LIVE WITH US.

Boy—age 10:

If I coud change my mom and dad I would have my dad come back to my family. If I could change them I would have then not get mad at me sometimes.

Girl — age 12:

change them to
be married
again and to
become
Christians

Boy — age 11:

I would make them like each other and not fight so much. I would like them to get married too.

Gail:

I wish my
dad was alive
and because he's
dead my mom
always gets
beat-up by her
boyfriend,

Boy:

I wish
my Dad
would Be
home.

One half of all children born in the United States will, at some time, live with only one parent. The primary reason, of course, is the escalating divorce rate. Fathers are walking away from their wives and children; women are leaving home to "find themselves" with new husbands or careers. Single parenthood has become an accepted social phenomenon.

When parents divorce, almost all children entertain the secret hope that their parents will be united again. Usually, the death of a parent is not as traumatic as a divorce. If the child feels he was loved by the deceased parent, he can accept the death. But if he feels rejected or responsible for the divorce, his emotional scars run deep.

Parents should never use children as weapons in a marital dispute. Regardless of who is at fault, a child should be taught to respect both parents. Parents who speak well of one another—no matter what happens—teach their children love and respect, rather than hate and disrespect.

The foundation for a solid marriage is built in childhood. If biblical values are not taught in the home, seeds are sown for the disintegration of another family in the next generation. A fractured family produces fractured children who tend to perpetuate the disobedience of their parents. Although God's grace can reverse the trend and break the cycle, statistics do confirm the cause-effect relationship.

Marriage partners can only be rightly related to each other when they are rightly related to God. The strongest marriages cannot survive unless the partners have learned the painful lessons of forgiveness. The best marriages are those that form a triangle between God, the husband, and the wife. Christ holds a home together, making it a rich and pleasant oasis.

9

Children Want Parents to Be Spiritual Leaders

Shepherd the flock of God among you, exercising oversight not under compulsion, but voluntarily . . . with eagerness . . . proving to be examples to the flock.

1 Peter 5:2-3

Girl—age 16:

I would make them people who *fully* trust God through *anything*. ... not just through good times. - not just "half"- Christians.

I wish they'd try to understand me better

girl—age 9:

If I could change my mom and dad. I would like my dad to become a christian. he goes to church but he doen't listen or sing. he just sits and thinks about other things

Boy—age 9:

If I could cange my mom and Dad I would make them pray with me and tell me more about Jesus.

Boy—age 10:

If I could change my mom I would have my mom & Dad spend more time whith me in the Bible

Girl—age 9:

If I could change my Mom and Dad I would tell them to tell me lots of Bible Stories.

Girl—age 8:

If I could change my mom and dad this is what I would do. I would let them pray with me all the times I have a problem.

girl—age 10:

I would change my Dad so that he would see that he needs christ. I would make my mom believe that my Dad would become a christian. I believe that he will with alot of your help + Gods help.

Amen!

Boy—age 12:

If I could change my mom & dad I would change them into christians because my mom and Dad don't Know christ. I try to tell them but it's just impossible.

Girl — age 16:

My parent are vantasic people but I wish that they could belief in the lord more then they do. I wish they could see how great the lord really is!

Children are more perceptive spiritually than we tend to recognize. They expect certain responses from their parents. To them, Christianity is not going to church or reading the Bible; it is the life that is lived in the home.

Children accept the Bible's message very seriously. My own children have at times expressed great concern about people who don't know Christ. A child is logical: If unsaved people are going to hell, then we ought to tell everyone we can about Jesus so that they will go to heaven. If parents believe in Christ but fail to witness, the child simply is not able to understand or tolerate their inconsistency.

The public school system in the United States is fraught with a lack of discipline. The price of peer acceptance is participation in such "adult" practices as sex and drugs. The sense of belonging is more powerful than any urge. Parents must compensate for the negative social influences found in school by active involvement in the church. Only through establishing solid friendships in church can a child withstand the peer pressure. Without that support the children, humanly speaking, have no chance of spiritual survival.

Children who say that they want their parents to become Christians may already have Christian parents but not know it! To a child, the fact that a person has received Christ as his Savior is, in itself, no evidence of the Christian life. If a child hears someone swear, sees someone inattentive at church, or witnesses an adult temper tantrum, he will automatically conclude that the person is not a

Christian. The words we speak and the lives we live must be consistent.

Are you a Christian at home as well as at church?

10

Some Children Are Satisfied with Their Parents

Children, obey your parents in the Lord, for this is right. HONOR YOUR FATHER AND MOTHER (which is the first commandment with a promise), THAT IT MAY BE WELL WITH YOU, AND THAT YOU MAY LIVE LONG ON THE EARTH.

Ephesians 6:1-3

girl—age 15:

If I could change
my mom or dad.
I don't really
think I'd change
them cause they
both love me &
they show it.
I can't even
think of one thing
that I would change.
Cause I love my
mom & dad both.

Girl – age 11:

I wouldn't want to change them because I love them the way they are. They're kind of strict but that is O.K. with me. They don't spoil me and I'm glad. My mom and dad are their own selves and they can always be the way they are.

Boy—age 11:

I wouldn't, no way, even if they do punish me sometimes. I still Love them And they Love Me.

Girl—age 10:

I wouldn't want to ~~chang~~ change my mom ~~or~~ and dad because they are christians and love the lord and thats all that ~~[illegible]~~ counts.

Girl — age 13:

I wouldn't change
one thing
about my parents,
for they are
both Christians
and we are
all content with
eachother

Boy—age 11:

If I could change my mom + Dad I would'nt change them they're just right.

Boy—age 14:

1. If I could change my mom and Dad I would not. Be cause God has put them over me just the way they are.

Girl—age 14:

If I could change my mom & Dad, <u>I wouldn't</u> because I love them just the way they are and them love me with all their heart and I would trade them for <u>anything ever</u>!

Not all children would change their moms and dads—even if they could!

Why are some genuinely satisfied? They are secure in their parents' love. Contentment! What a tribute to the life-style and values of their parents!

1. A child must be assured that his parents accept him independently of his performance. He is not loved only if he does well at school or if he doesn't embarrass his parents. He needs to feel he is on the top of his parents' list of values.

2. Respect and love are two different things. Parents who love their children often communicate disrespect for them in subtle ways, by belittling a child or thinking he is more trouble than he is worth. Children need to know that their opinions and feelings count when parents make decisions. Respect must accompany love.

3. Although most parents think that children abhor discipline, if a vote were taken children would agree that they seek the security consistent discipline can bring. Creative and consistent discipline takes thought, prayer, and wisdom—signs of parents who care.

4. Children look to their parents for examples of moral and spiritual values. A child wants to be proud of his mom and dad. He wants to know that they are concerned for the ultimate values that Christians cherish. Despite their resentment and complaining, young people do want and respect parents who continue faithfully in their walk with the Lord despite the difficulties of life.

Perhaps the greatest compliment a parent can receive is for his child to say, "If I could change my mom and dad, I wouldn't!"

Conclusion: A Child and His God

At that time the disciples came to Jesus, saying, "Who then is greatest in the kingdom of heaven?" And He called a child to Himself and set him before them . . . . "Whoever then humbles himself as this child, he is the greatest in the kingdom of heaven."

Matthew 18:1-2, 4

Mark Allen Lust became ill with leukemia at the age of four. He died six years later. Mark was bright, good-looking, and energetic. He enjoyed most of the activities the other boys did but had to give them up one by one as his illness progressed. While he was ill he experienced some serious thinking far beyond his years. He often thought about eternity, God, and heaven, and he spoke freely about his sickness and impending death.

Mark loved church and was distressed when he became unable to continue attending. He learned to pray with a fervent and believing heart. Mark's grandmother's account of his life said:

> Our Mark was a boy who loved the Lord from the time he was a little baby and could only look at pictures and hear his mommy or daddy say, "This is Jesus." Later when he could read he spent much time in prayer and study of the Bible. His Bible was well marked with verses he had committed to memory.
>
> He and his God had an understanding about health problems. He had talked so long and so earnestly with the Lord about healing. He said, "I got down to business with the Lord last night and I told Him if He is not going to heal me to tell me and to tell me why." He dropped the matter there and said no more but we all knew that he and his God had it all worked out together. Two weeks before he died he told his mother that he was going to die but he was not afraid to meet his God.
>
> He had a very long prayer list, and everyone whom he met was added. He prayed for

the doctors, nurses, cleaning women, and anyone else who entered his hospital room. After he was gone, some of the nurses and a Jewish doctor came to the funeral home. I asked whether they usually did this and the doctor replied, "No, but Mark was a very special little Christian." One of the verses underlined in his Bible was, "Enoch walked with God and was not for God took him." Well, that's what happened to our little Mark.

Can a child know God? Ponder again Christ's words in Matthew 18: "whoever causes one of these little ones *who believe in Me* to stumble. . ." (v. 6, italics added). Little ones *can* believe in Him. Charles Haddon Spurgeon said, "When a child knowingly sins, he can savingly believe." Although it is possible for children to make a shallow decision for Christ out of fear of punishment or desire for reward, we must remember that children can indeed grasp the key concepts of the gospel.

1. Remember to talk about God's willingness to forgive sins. A child will understand that he has been naughty and needs forgiveness. Children misunderstand religious symbolism and terminologies, because they are literalists, but if a child is taught to forgive others, then he will understand God's forgiveness.

2. Key theological concepts should be reinforced by example. Like God's forgiveness, Christ's death *for us* could be understood by illustrations drawn from everyday life.

3. Parents who lay a careful foundation of scriptural truth will discover that the Holy Spirit will bring

a child to the point of decision. Be sensitive to notice when a child is ready to transfer his trust to Christ for the forgiveness of sins.

4. Remember that saving faith is an act of trust, not a prayer. You may want to lead your child in prayer when he trusts Christ as Savior, but don't assume he is saved simply because he has said the right words. Thus, if the child has doubts in later years, don't hesitate to ask him whether he is indeed trusting Christ for his salvation. At that time, with a deeper understanding, he may be better prepared to make that transfer of trust.

There is no doubt that God reveals Himself to little children. We must do what we can to plant the right seeds. In good time they will germinate and lead to everlasting life.

Surely nothing is as beautiful as a child and his God!

Moody Press, a ministry of the Moody Bible Institute, is designed for education, evangelization, and edification. If we may assist you in knowing more about Christ and the Christian life, please write us without obligation: Moody Press, c/o MLM, Chicago, Illinois 60610.